THE Unleashable DOG

CHARLES RAFFERTY

THE
Unleashable
DOG

CHARLES
RAFFERTY

STEEL TOE
B O O K S
Bowling Green,
Kentucky

ISBN 978-0-9824169-9-0

STEEL TOE BOOKS
Western Kentucky University
Department of English
1906 College Heights Blvd. #11086
Bowling Green, KY 42101-1086
steeltoebooks.com

COVER PHOTOGRAPH
Wendy Rafferty

COVER AND BOOK DESIGN
Molly McCaffrey

STEEL TOE BOOKS is affiliated with Western Kentucky University.

For Wendy, Callan, and Chatham

TABLE OF Contents

I. SATISFACTIONS

II. FRUSTRATIONS

III. ANTICIPATIONS

Satisfactions

ONE

THE MAN WITH A HAWK IN HIS SUITCASE

He has always enjoyed traveling — the smell
of other continents, the street-side food,
the noises of women in his rented bed.
But he dreads unpacking — the wild
batting of the hawk as it crashes
about the room in search of a perch up high.
He has learned to open the bathroom first,
for the bird prefers a shower rod, and of course
it must be fed — with mice if he can get them
or with a sandwich of local meat.
When he brings a woman back to his room,
she is wary of the restrained fury
that stares down at her as she pees.
And as she and the man make love,
there is always the chance the hawk will
mistake her tossing hair for an animal
in distress. The woman wants to leave
when that happens, or rather, she flees
into the corridor, wrapped only in talon marks
and fear. It is always the same.
The man hands her crumpled dress
through the half-opened door
while the bird knocks over table lamps
and shreds the curtains. When the man is told
to leave, the hawk goes willingly
into the suitcase. The bird allows him
to wedge it like a shoe into the last
available space. Then he's on his way back
to his dutiful wife and children, their stylish house,

their garden and their yard, and beyond that,
the flat and grassy fields through which
something is always moving,
catching the eye of the last living thing
it will ever have occasion to touch.

APPETITES

When he gets home she is drinking
from the aquarium, and as she brushes the hair back
to give him her face hello,

he swears he can see the ragged fin
of a damselfish sucked in. What kind of woman is this —
who eats his fish in secret, whose salty kiss

he's starting to understand? There was a time
when her nails were tipped with black crescents.
Days later he discovered the scoop marks

where her fingers had been in the dirt
of his potted palms. Another time
her mouth had tasted like dimes

and he regretted the coin collection —
the little gods and Indians that lived
underneath his socks. Suddenly he has an explanation

for his missing keys, the remote control,
the photos in the album removed like words
in a steady redaction of his past.

Could she really have been swallowing his life
while he kissed her hard
and paid the bills? He remembers

her penchant for negligees
and dirty stories, the arch of her body
above him. And there it is. His breath

devoured, without effort or malice,
as if it were the plaything
of a woman grown bored

who hasn't come round to cruelty.

THE MAN WITH A MISSING DOG

One evening, while searching for a dog
that had squeezed beneath its fence,
I came across a couch with its legs knocked off
in the center of a field — as if someone intended
to click through the channels
of maple and scarlet oak. The couch
had been dragged through jewelweed and prickers,
when someone decided that a hundred feet
behind the strip mall was far enough.
It had been there for months, maybe years.
There were beer cans and condoms, countless cigarettes,
a pile of ash dispersed — and a sapling
driven like a nail between the cushions
that the earth kept pounding up.
No one would recline on a couch like this —
its stuffing erupting and full of dirt.
But somebody did. Somebody had a good time
out in the goldenrod and shade. I thought of the girl
who must have been there — how she opened
like a gift, how she redeemed the blasted upholstery,
how she overcame a field of random trash
with the traffic blurring by — the glow
of the Mobil station lighting the steps
she took on the way back out. It was private —
a place that no one frequented but high school lovers
and runaway dogs. Good for her, I thought —
to make use of her body and this palsied couch
before it became worthless to all but the mice
and millipedes. But it was getting late.

I saw where the path continued and I took it.
Somewhere up ahead the unleashable dog
had begun its nightly barking.

THE MAN WITH A STAR ON THE TIP OF EACH FINGER

After the eleven o'clock news
he clicks off the table lamp and touches
his wife. The light from his fingers
is tentative, the tips of them scarlet
in the blanketed dark. Above them — beyond
their roof, the tarpaulin of clouds,
and the blinding moon — the real stars
go unnoticed. This is always the case.
The stars above are a failure — no match
for the floodlights and motion sensors
hanging from every eave. So tonight
she is illumined and burned
by the constellation of his embrace,
the way it seizes her into the infinite
permutations of his touch. She becomes
a sky for him to climb inside,
a place for him to put his stars
as he coaxes her darkness down.

THEORY

If we lived each day
as if it were our last, we'd never
get anything done.

Can taxes
or snow tires ever supersede
the honey of a girl?

We would eat the foods
that hurt us: rare pork, blowfish,
the sizzling fat

of anything —
everywhere the concussion
of mediocre wine

pushing us down
to the couch. The piano would be
left untuned, the children

unvaccinated,
my haircut put off until I became
at last a shaggy corpse

that no one will bury,
because the mortician won't
answer

his phone, as he works
like a rat at the hooks of your bra.
You won't even ask

if his hands are clean.

THE MAN BENEATH THE JANUARY STARS

He wakes so early the summer constellations
are up and making mischief
in the blasted maples — the light seeming
out of place because it's never been
this clear. In summer, the horizon was
always fringed with a remnant
of thunderstorm, the humidity crowding
the duller stars out — the way
these maples obscure his neighbors
at the summit of August heat.
These out-of-place stars get him thinking
of the Naugatuck coursing beneath its ice,
the purple blood of the rhododendrons
hiding in their roots, waiting
to open like lovely wounds we can only
collect and vase. The summer night
will never be as brilliant as this
bitter and pre-dawn sky —
the air bereft of crickets and whippoorwills,
the only sound the tiny thunder
of a jetliner already passed.

THE MAN WITH A MISSING WATCH IN SPRING

He isn't sure where he dropped it, but he'd better
find it soon. Already the flags
of poison ivy are rising from the rot
of the backyard woods. Already
the maples are popping open
their million small umbrellas
to blot the bluing sky. Somewhere,
among the rank moisture of the morning
and the dawn's caroling desire,
his Bulova glints like a piece of money
or trash. If anything, the world is trying
to cover it up — to grime it with moss,
to shade it with something more intricate
and commonplace than an Eifel Tower,
a statue by Rodin. No one takes the time, it seems,
to notice so many masterpieces
hauling themselves aloft: mourning cloak
and hickory leaf, the rash of violets
spreading all over his lawn. And this
is the week when each of them is perfect — before
the caterpillars and droughts, the leaf molds
and blights, the prolonged exposure
to air and sun. Yes, this is the week with a missing
watch. But it's also the week
when a man can't bother to get on his knees
in search of anything but what has been rising
to stop him with gold and green.

THE MAN WITH ROTTEN FRUIT ON HIS WRIST

Each morning he straps a piece of it on
where someone else would put a watch.
He goes to work and a woman on the train
compliments his cologne. *It's very citrusy,*
she says. The sleeve of his overcoat
is hiding the rotten lime, and he accepts
her praise with a smile, a little tip
of his chin. At work he has to be careful.
Already the watermelon juice he dribbled
on his keyboard has made the space bar
unreliable. If it's a banana, a tiny cloud of fruit flies
sings above his wrist, and his officemates
often complain. When someone asks
for the time, he looks at the browned apple core
and says it's later than he thought,
that there's no time for tasting like yesterday.
All summer he is followed by wasps. They dance
on the fruit like acrobatic clock hands.
When asked why he straps old fruit to his wrist,
he says simply that ash is impractical,
that fog forgets to linger. Besides, he likes always
being ready to boo a performance
or to plant a small garden at the end of the world.

THE MAN WITH A CARDINAL IN HIS BEDROOM

He wakes to a scarlet commotion
above his bed — a bird unable to distinguish
the three-inch crack of air where it had entered
from the glass it finds repeatedly.
When the cardinal tires, the man is
able to scoop it off his sheets. He feels
the fluttering heart-heat of a bird
so bright it almost seems fake —
as if some kid had painted it,
as if it came from some other continent
and would not be able to live
among his looming and everyday oaks. But no,
the cardinal is common here.
It thrives just out of reach in the branches
beyond his room, filling the man's mornings
with the rung metal of its call,
and as he cradles it to the window, he feels
how easily he could snuff its tiny flame.
But then he opens his hands outside
and the bird explodes, leaving a tail feather
in his palm, a smear of runny shit. All day
the man thinks of the bird as it bit into his thumb
with a brilliant beak, how he had stared
into the black ball bearings of its eyes —
both of them refusing to flinch.

THE MAN DESCRIBES THE END OF HIS ESCAPE

The yard is soft with melting. I leave
deep tracks in the grassless mud
between the back door and the trash cans.
If I were a fugitive, I'd be easy

to follow — no need for bloodhounds
and helicopters, just an overweight sheriff
with a gun he's willing to use.
It's the kind of landscape that forces you

to turn. And that's what I find myself
suddenly wanting, ready
to confront that which has followed me for years
through the slackening pace

of my escape. I need to make sense
of the hands that held me, the problem
of being locked and loving it —
the body's unleaveable jail.

A RAPTURE THAT FOLLOWED AUGUST RAIN

I had left you
in the bed, the sunset suddenly
ablaze. It was as if

the sky were wine
and I'd had a glass too much of it.
Then the reeling began.

Under my shirt
that bruise in the shape
of a bombed-out

cathedral didn't hurt
anymore — the oldest parts
were gold. In the garden

the petunias
were damp in their dirt. If I walked
among them I would have left

footprints. Those purple
sores were untouchable. Already
I was rising like the flame

of something fanned.
Starlings called from the crowns
of dripping oaks,

as if to hurry my ascent.

THE DISAPPEARING MAN

The disappearing man was almost gone.
He looked as though he'd been
silk-screened onto the air
and faded more with every door
that shut inside his house.
He wanted to end things, but he couldn't
pinch up the bullets. The trigger
was unpullable anyway by the fog
of finger he had left. Besides
he'd rather strum it against his wife
as if she were a mandolin, a thing
he could hold and tune, a thing he could turn
into April birds. After he disappeared
for good, his wife stopped waiting
for the bread she'd put on his list,
but the man continued
to live with her even as she took
a new lover and replaced
the chandelier he nearly broke
his neck installing. He became
the dust, the air, the angled light,
the disruption in her bedroom curtains
whenever he tried to reach her. It made her
think of old-time movie theaters
when, as a girl, she'd sneak inside —
that jiggle in the velvet drapes
when the stagehands took hold of the ropes
and the show she had been
waiting for was ready to begin at last.

THE MAN WHO ENJOYS GETTING BLACKMAILED

It's the attention, really — that
and the photographs he finds underneath
his wiper blade as he comes back
to the car, his dry cleaning
spilling to the asphalt as he reaches
for the envelope. The photographer knows
his work. The woman is air-brushed
in a believably glamorous way,
and the venetian blind shadows
are an elegant motif. He understands
composition, the need to balance
the clove of her buttock
with the table lamp, the jacketed chair.
This is the second batch, and again
the photographs have exceeded his recollection.
He had no idea he was this
good, this passionate, this able to bring
a tax attorney to ecstasy
as he bent her over the writing desk
at the Bridgewater Holiday Inn.
He'd been there on business for the job
that keeps him fed, paralyzed
by bills he is almost able to pay.
The woman had said he was cute
and laughed sincerely at his drunken jokes.
It was that simple. And now
the letters are coming, demanding
payment, threatening to disclose
the truth of him, the shame. Is it

a boyfriend? A detective? A run-of-the-mill
extortionist who hangs out
on the balconies of cheap hotels
waiting for middle-aged alcoholics
to cheat on their dutiful wives? It doesn't matter —
he'll never pay. He wants his wife to see
what he can become in her hands —
if only she would mold him, if only
she would let him climb like this
into the sky above their bed.

THE PORNOGRAPHER SPEAKS

There is an art
to arranging a woman
like an overturned

vase of tulips,
a jigsaw puzzle
spilled

across a pool table —
her discarded
cocktail dress like a scrap

of glittering trash,
her body
ready for whatever

you might imagine.
The trick
is to make it seem

like she wanted you
to see her
like this. Before you turn

the page
you should think
you understand her

completely — the very
shade of her soul,
the pinkening quick

of her body.
If I've taken her right,
her smiles are pure

subversion. It's as if
she's watching you
through the keyhole

of the page —
in which she opens
suddenly

as an oyster,
with the twisting
of a blade. She is

unclosable now — a box
with a bent hinge,
a mouth

cracked apart
for the permanent
song

only I can make her sing.

BUTCHER

Think of the butcher — how he spends his days
cutting up animals his daughters would like
to pet. He cleavers chickens into more
priceable portions. He runs a calf through
a band saw, the frozen meat flying up
like murderous rain against his goggles.
It goes on like this all day, week in and week out.
Year after year he makes animals less
recognizable. He makes the shoulder meat
of anything cry out for the grill. Sometimes
people ring the little bell to call him out
from the large refrigerator that is his office.
What do they ask, I wonder. Is it possible
to mislabel steak so badly somebody might guess
it were eggs or cereal or holiday cards?
And his daughters — I can imagine the lies
he tells them: that the meat grows out of the ground
like corn, or that it's only the mean cows
he unloads from the truck behind his shop,
or that these animals died when their hair fell out
at the moment they learned how hungry they were.
His girls I mean — the ones sitting down
to a plate overpacked with porterhouse and flank.

THE MAN EXPLAINS HIS SOUVENIRS

Twenty years ago, the skeleton
of a wild pig gleamed among violets
while the leaf-rot around it
grew hot with spring. I slipped
the molar out of its grin like an oiled key
and took it home, leaving the boar
to reassemble, if it ever did,
at a gap-toothed resurrection. I hold it up
to show my daughters. They are less
impressed each year. I have antlers
and trilobites and chips of pretty bedrock
from all the places where the sun came up
to burn me awake with beauty — even
a turtle shell we used as an ashtray
in that first apartment, on the bank
of a creek that flooded every March
and took our trash to sea. All of it
sleeps in a basement box — a kind of coffin
for my former life, but also a proof
that I stooped to the world,
that I kept what came my way.

COMET

In West Virginia, we tumbled from the hotel bar
to see a comet overhead
like a chip of fog in the sequined dark.
Our first comet. It was stunning
for this alone. But where was the tail?
The wagging flames? What future
could this inspire? It was hard to see
how it could frighten a continent
or be blamed for any of history.
Somewhere within a block's radius
a magnolia tree was blooming,
the unmistakable stink of beauty.
We finished our drinks and fell to bed.
Early the next day, we headed back
for Connecticut — the sun unrisen,
the magnolia scent still splashing
the air like a recently ripped-up skunk.
The comet stayed with us for weeks —
slowly brightening as it climbed
into the horizon. Strange how it never
exceeded the grandeur
of that first night in West Virginia.
It is the same with love and death, I think —
the powerful talisman
of the first nude woman or the first empty bed,
how we can't stop sleeping with either.

TWO
Frustrations

THE MAN WITH A SHIRT OF FIRE

It wakes him up — the glow of his shirt
hanging in the bedroom closet,
the light leaking from beneath a door
that doesn't quite want to close.
He is always thinking of a girl at such times,
the uneaten peach of her, the wetness
of where he might bite. The same light
follows him on midnight walks, a glare
that prevents him from enjoying
even the sharpest stars. Come morning
he takes down the shirt and buttons
around himself the familiar agony.
He knows it cannot be put out: The meadow
will blaze up if he rolls in the breeze
of its many fingers. The bouquet he picks
will droop and crisp before he can
make his way to her. Every night,
coming home alone, suffused with wine,
he is orbited by moths that flutter
and die beneath the million stars he has
never seen. He smells faintly of destruction,
the way a burnt-down house asserts itself
after even a misting of rain.

THE MAN IN CHARGE OF DARKNESS

For a while he spent his time adding it
to bourbon, the back seats of cars
so lovers could have some privacy
in the Foodtown parking lot. He squeezed it
into clock hands and guitar wood, dabbed
an indelible drop of it at the center
of each woman's eye. But he had to waste
whole pails of it as he did up
the space between the stars,
and sometimes the brush would tremor
in his hand and a star went out forever.
If anyone noticed, he never heard about it.
This bothered him. His mistakes
and the world's complacency taught him
he didn't much matter, that light
was abundant and forever confounding
the essence of his work. He hated
children with night lights. He hated the woman
down the street who lit up
her stand of 2 a.m. cedars, confusing
the profound with the merely pretty. He remembered
when he first wanted the job — after breaking
his last flashlight in the belly of a cave.
He'd never felt more crucial — that darkness
made his mind meander, it made his fingers
mean it as they groped over the rocks
around him. He had to lick his lips to tell
where the cave wind came from.
But the darkness he works with now seems

less serious, almost frivolous. He gives it
to the worms to thread through their corpses.
He gives it to the owls to hold it fast
between the midnight branch and talon.
His only consolation is his own shadow,
how it withstands the reading lamp, the gibbous moon.
Even at night there is always a darkness
darker than the rest, and it cannot be cast off.

THE MAN WITH A WOMAN WAITING

The car ends up on a shoulder so narrow
he has to get out on the passenger side.

It is one of those breakdowns
where everything on his dashboard

lights up briefly before going black —
coasting him to this one bad place.

It is under an overpass though,
and the blur of the storm gives way

to the clarity of shivering damp.
He listens to the hundred pigeons

conspiring in the crowded I-beams,
the sizzle of the rain on the road.

The horns are louder here. Of course
he has no phone to call the woman

he was headed for, no umbrella,
no hint of rescue. There is only the promise

of a long wet walk, or the failure
of not moving now

in the direction of her waiting – her body
laid out like a gleaming wrench

that would tighten the man it touched.

THE MAN WITH A BOAT AT THE BOTTOM OF THE LAKE

It was a small boat. It had kissed some rocks
and grown unbalanced. It ended
belly-up in the calm waters
of the after-storm, the ivory hull
shining faintly at a depth
of twenty feet. He likes to swim
above it, to inspect it — sometimes
with the clear eyes of a mask
tightened to his face, sometimes
with the blurred intimacy
of his eyes pressed into the lake.
Some days he sits on the rocks
that sank her — gathering heat
from the sun before plummeting in.
He's thought about going down all the way.
He started to once but he felt
his ears cracking. He knows
he could get there quickly by hugging
a boulder and diving from a raft,
but he worries about the speed
of floating back empty-armed.
Thus, the things he once imagined saving
remain on the bottom: his fishing tackle,
the decorative anchor, the name
on the side the same as the girl he used
to love, the strangled motor
that growled when he told it to, the feel
of the wheel within his hands that threatened
to take him anywhere he looked

on that vast and glittering lake —
a world so bright he could only see it
by almost closing his eyes.

THE PROBLEM WITH ALMANACS

On the map, Kansas is pink — an almost
rectangle with a corner torn off.
It reminds me of the smooth inside curl
of a conch or of a woman,
or of certain orchids that grow in jungles
where the frogs are poisonous
and the cats can kill you, or of a sunset
so colossal cars pull over to take it in —
heedless of errands and dinner dates,
the evening news and its ads
for antidepressants. But the almanac
talks only of wheat and corn, the average
reported land values per acre,
by type and district. It breaks
the population down by income
and followed god. No matter the pie chart,
there is no statistic for the beauty
that must be there, no explanation
for so many roads crisscrossing the page
I am suddenly wanting to turn.

THE OCEAN AT THE END OF OUR STREET

It was there after we stayed up making love
in the 2 a.m. light of the television set.

It was there on the patio where one of us went
whenever we'd had a fight. It was there

in the dawn in a glory of gulls — a vastness,
a churning, a landscape we could taste.

The beaches were built of trucked-in sand.
If we walked the line where the tide gave up,

we could see the sand didn't match
from one end of town to the next — shifting

from tan to an almost pink to a block
of windy rust. Whenever we swam in it,

the bottom ran away into rocks
and cold water, and everything wore down

in that cradle of sloshing grays: whelks
and beer bottles, wharf pilings. All summer

the party boats cruised offshore — the just-right
wind taking to the beach a stray guitar,

the clinking of ice in a single glass,
but never the song entire, never the gin itself

with its wedge of puckering lime. Month after month,
the moon rose up like a lopsided peach

that threatened to fall back down, while the ocean
stayed big and kept its promise

to polish the pieces of our breaking world.

LOBSTER

My friend the ex-smoker says he was
at the grocery store once, the seafood section,
peering into the giant aquarium
where they keep the lobsters. One of them
had popped the rubber band from his claw
and was attacking his brothers:
antennae, eyestalks, and a score of little legs
floated among the tumult. And there was one
finger-crushing claw pinched off at the base,
rising and falling whenever one moved.
A dozen lobsters lived in the tank — packed enough
so that one of them was always walking
over the others. The lobster on the rampage wasn't
the biggest — but my friend said he got the sense
that he'd been walked on with impunity
from the moment he'd been seduced
by the rotting cod of the lobster pot. For years
he'd lived on the bottom, devouring the shit
of everything beautiful as it floated down
to meet him. And now he was here
under the fluorescent sky of a grocery store —
surrounded by the tapping of children,
people peering in with the weekend's party
shining in their eyes. The fishman was out
by the back door smoking a cigarette.
When my friend waved him in, he pretended
he didn't see, took one step farther out.
My friend couldn't afford lobster anyway
and, having recently quit smoking, wanted

no parts of a person still in its thrall.
He watched for another minute
as the broken parts tried to settle. It was bittersweet.
He knew the freed lobster would be the first
one sold. After all, people like their lobsters intact
before setting them adrift in the bubbling pot
and, later, cracking into them
to sweeten the dead with butter.

THE MAN ON BREAK

She's waiting for me inside, patient,
letting me finish the cigarette
I've treated myself to beside the giant doors
where the ambulance always backs up
without any of its spinning lights.
When I go in, I'll rubber-glove myself
and crack her open — to cut and weigh,
to sample and stain. Her dead heart
in my hands won't say anything I couldn't
guess. She's young, probably drugs. I tell the cops
not to mention anything about how
they find the bodies. It's a game I play
with myself — like crosswords or solitaire.
Later, perhaps, they'll show me her note,
the gin-smeared script of her good-bye.
I'll stitch her up tight for the family's sake —
who wait with a marble patience
so they can hide her in the ground
this weekend. It's the same ground I see
all over town — the borders of lawns
bursting with daffodils, and the lawns
themselves like damp emeralds.
It's obscene. This is my proof for god
having abandoned us. Why wouldn't he
reach his great finger down to this girl
as if he were gluing the handle
back on a teacup? He either can't or won't —
both of which disqualify him from anything
approaching praise. When I smoke this down,

I'll return to the table I've set for her —
the silvery utensils lined up,
the halogen lights ready to cancel
the shadow she can't stop making.

THE MAN DESCRIBES THEIR FAILED VACATION

By some mistake of money and advice
we ended up at Hilton Head in August —
a week beside blue water
where everyone else was old. They wanted us
to believe in their paradise
of guided tours, talking about golf
and television, the price
of medication. We were twenty-seven,
and by Wednesday we had to get out of town,
to escape the raked sand of the beaches,
the violins piped out of the hotel ferns.
It was over a hundred at the nature preserve,
so hot we almost couldn't care
that a thousand fiddler crabs the size of dimes
clicked into the mud at our approach.
The locals had filled us with talk
of alligators and fire ants,
and as we were looking at a flower glued shut
with its own nectar, the only snake
I've never tried to pick up
drifted by in the grass so close to us,
and with such carelessness,
I worried what else was near. The week
wasn't over. We had yet to enter
the shop that sold seascapes,
the shop that sold facsimiles
of maritime antiques. A series
of restaurants we couldn't afford
awaited our reservations. Here and there,

in the trees we could not name,
the herons stared into us, ragged and white,
too heavy with heat to fly.

FAMILY VACATION

Toward the end of it, we stopped
for a sudden roadside zoo. There wasn't much
to see in that broiling August noon:
the tail of a tiger immobile
in tall grass, a monkey whose temper was such
we left believing he deserved his cage.
And an elephant, too, that children could ride —
five dollars for a turn around the dust
he'd been stampeding for the last ten years.
Some of the exhibits were empty —
just scattered straw, the water bowls
smeared with dung. At the food court
even the adults were misbehaving:
demanding manners from the bored
and toddling, refusing their desserts.
Only the petting zoo goats were a triumph —
so willing to be touched, to not bite back.
Later, when the last cage had been peered into
and failed to satisfy whatever people want
when they look at captured animals,
one family after another strapped
themselves in to their screaming vans
and fled. They headed for the ocean,
the mountains, the invincible myth of Maine
and how it will always be wild.

ROCK COLLECTION

My mother brought me a dozen stones
from an Alaskan beach — pink and gray ovals
that brightened when I wet them.
They were paralyzed for years in a glass bowl
on the knick-knack shelf, until my daughter
found them and began mixing them
with the stones my father had brought
from Ireland, and the stones I had
from Arkansas and Maine, and all the stones
people had given me from Africa
and Spain. They were not spectacular —
just little eggs of color that could fit
inside a pocket, the tiniest pouch
of a travel bag. Once they were all together,
I couldn't tell whether they came from Alaska
or my own back yard. So in a fit of order,
I flung them as far as I could
into the woods behind our house.
I regretted this even before their small
stampede had stalled among autumn leaves.
I would miss the clack of them
in my daughter's hands, how she'd pretend
they were planets or jewels lined up
on the living room floor. Now, the largeness
of Alaska is lost in suburban woods —
among the tree forts and the graves of pets,
the lights of my neighbor's porch at night
so bright they kill the stars.

ON BEING ASKED IF I'D EVER BEEN TO GEORGIA

I had a fifteen-minute layover in Atlanta,
headed from one place full of desire
to another bereft of all. I remember the lights
of the city as we banked above it —
a vast and toppled Christmas tree
no one had bothered to right.
Later, I chuffed through the wide hallways —
refusing the smiles of the greeters,
demanding the path to the place my ticket
insisted that I be. There wasn't even time
for a drink before I got in the line
and left. Sometimes, I wonder
about that Georgia dirt I never walked on.
For all I know it is made of watch cogs
and glitter. I have only the mulch of the airport
planters, which dotted my route
through the artificial air of a terminal
that shunted me back into sky.
On the plane, I was shown the escape routes,
and the lights of the world became small
and untouchable once again. Up ahead,
the stewardess and her cart of little whiskeys
came closer row by row.

THE MAN WHOSE FRIENDS HAD RISEN

One evening, my friends called from the top
of Colorado. Two time zones away,
it was light on Mt. Elbert — the only storm
still distant, the temperature holding.
They said they might have an hour
before things got dangerous, and they were
giddy. Someone was opening wine
in the background because their view
wasn't possible back east. They said
they would descend, that they would hunker
in tents where the trees began
beside a fire of their own making.
It was darkening outside my own window,
the blaze of autumn maples invisible,
the baby crying from another room
for my wife's delicious body. I was straddled
by small mountains. My friends
had no children of their own, and couldn't
understand how hard I took their call.
A job that didn't love me waited
at the end of the driveway, and I stepped outside
as the baby settled into my wife. All around me
the blackness gathered in our valley,
and I looked for the night's first stars,
the ones that had always failed
to make even the smallest difference.

DESCENT

We woke with hangovers on the steep side
of a mountain, the blackbirds and jays
screaming, the last snowdrifts hiding
in the permanent shade above our camp.
The first things were in flower,
the ground sopping. The night before it was all
planets and constellations, a fire to keep us talking.
Now the difficulty of fitting things back
inside their packs, the immense puzzle
of gear and whiskey-addled hands. Down below
our car was parked on a gravel road.
If it had a name, we didn't know it. We limped for it
like wounded fools, repeating the path
that had taken us into clouds. In the valley
a radio would tell us about errant grenades,
the festering Intifada, the missiles corroding
on a Russian base where the doors
were never locked. It was the same story
we'd been hearing for years
and a little worse because of it —
a hundred languages and a handful of gods
refusing to give up anything. We were no better.
We had mortgages and jobs and children
who believed in whatever we said.
Our temples were throbbing now.
Somebody remarked how the night before
they counted more satellites than shooting stars.
The rest of us nodded. We checked the map.
We headed for the place our car should be.

THE RISING

It's one of those moments when you're on
the highway, crossing a city's limits,
and the tallest buildings ignite
with the dawn behind you, so that it looks

like you're charging into a larger sunrise
built from thousands of brassy windows.
It's painful. The traffic slows. You turn off
the news to keep from crashing.

And then, with a slight angling of the road,
the blindness is gone, the city itself again —
and you continue speeding south, tempted
to return for a glimpse of that gold

and its glorious disorientation. But you know
it would be missing by the time
you doubled back. The city would churn
the way it always has, and then

you'd remember that your muffler needs
work, that it's been months
since you made love to the woman
you're sleeping with, that you're headed

for a desk that overlooks other desks —
lined up behind windows
unopenable by design, the spider plants
thriving despite your care.

LOVE AT THE STAMFORD TRANSPORTATION CENTER

There's a bouquet of tulips jammed
flower-sides down in a giant ashtray,
and some pigeons are fucking
on the far end of the platform. All around

the traffic and trains and buses
are seething in the quitting-time light
of an early evening with rain. The prettiest girl
in the station refuses to return

anyone's lechery, which is only
half-hearted, given this crowd
of demolished accountants and editors
sucking their cigarettes —

their train-time beers in little bags
that crackle as they shift and huddle.
Just two people in this hive
of departures seem truly happy.

They are young and embracing
on the opposite platform — a pile of baggage
behind them — French kissing so deeply
and in so public a place it can only be sincere.

For the rest of us, the problem of destination
intrudes like the rain slanting underneath
the narrow roofs that are everywhere
and useless — or like this loudspeaker,

saying that our train has now arrived,
that the lovers we've been
watching will not be boarding,
that they'll only get smaller as we travel

to a place they think they'll never be.

AN EPIPHANY DURING THE MORNING TRAFFIC ON I-95

The woman in my rearview mirror
refuses to meet my eyes.
She fusses with the radio, her cigarettes,
the mascara made possible
by heavy traffic. She seems instead
to be looking at the eyes
behind her, and I know it will always
be this way: the world back there
laying claim to our attention
merely by existing, the world up ahead
all exits and appointments,
people to pay or avoid. I'd like to stop
right here, to shoulder my door open
and greet the world full on
as it honks its way toward me
like an angry and injured goose.
But this is not what happens.
Wherever we are, we keep at least one hand
on the wheel, each of us
listening hard to the music
of our separate cars. It can make us feel
almost anything. And though she is the branch
beneath my sparrow, the shelf
that holds my whiskey, the centuries
that push this moment up
on the shining point of a pin, the woman
aloft in my rearview mirror
will never understand
I am singing these words for her.

THE MAN LAMENTS THE BEES THAT DIDN'T STING

A swarm of honeybees veered into the reception,
alighting on the canvas ceiling
of the bridal tent. The huddle of bees was big
as a carving station ham, mumbling
above the bar. Everyone fled of course. The band laid down
their red guitars, the bridesmaids scooted in
with a rabble of ugly cousins underneath another tent,
and the bartender refused to mix more drinks
beneath a frothing ball of bees.
When the beekeeper got there, everyone cheered
his ridiculous suit, the little gun
that shot smoke and stupor. The bride was all
but forgotten as he climbed
his tipsy ladder, scooped the bees
into an old UPS box, and drove off with that fury
in his pickup bed — as if he had selected
the best present from the sagging table of gifts
and made off with it unimpeded — something vital
that everyone would miss decades later
when they told the story of the bees again.
No one was stung. That was the problem.
The bees could have sent people dancing
into the koi pond, or under the skirted dessert cart,
or into the arms of lovers who couldn't
do anything anyway. Instead there was
a bee man and an armload of bees
apparently happy to assume the shape
of whatever box he opened.

THE LESSON OF LESS LIGHT

Our friend's airplane screamed into the sky
at twilight. After a minute the engine sound disappeared
and he was off to his spectacular life
of New York City bars and women
with complicated underwear. The good life.
You and I had been squabbling, a matter made worse
because we had no chance to voice
our small complaints — the old problem
of a single bedroom with company
that overstays. Driving home from the Tulsa airport
we saw the farms get bigger, the farmhouses less frequent,
the kudzu poised to take the shape
of whatever was in its path: fence line,
telephone poles, stand of crippled oaks.
It was a kind of resurrection
and a long ride back. Then it was moonless,
the road carless except for us —
the sky scraped free of jets and men.
We ended up stopping on the shoulder
of a road whose name I don't recall,
though at the time I'm sure we fought about it —
the map, directions, speed. One of us had to pee.
Probably you. So I cut the headlights
and we stepped outside. There was a farmhouse jammed
into the land a mile away — one light on
in each end of it, a gulf of blackness
uncrossable in between. Our eyes adjusted
and then the sky insisted it was ours —
the Milky Way a storm of light,

the closer stars like nailheads holding up
the night. We had never seen so many,
living as we did in the concussed air
of streetlamp, mall, and interchange.
It was the kind of sky that doesn't want you
to get back in and drive. But we had someplace to be,
an argument to finish. This is how
we failed the lesson of less light
and how it helps you see.

THREE
Anticipations

THE MAN WHO IS READY

I'm on the brink of daffodils.
The backyard snow is full of urine
blooms, the mud underneath is ready
to be itself. It won't be long
before the planet tilts and the birds
roll north like marbles, the sap
crawls out of the bedrock. The meadow's
sublimation makes me feel
like a piece of sky — ready to plummet,
ready to rain. Up on the mountain
the snowcap wishes toward water —
a wildness that doesn't lose pace,
no matter the stones crowding its path,
no matter the roots of everything. Down here
I'm waiting for the ants to arrive
with their shifting script, their message
from below. I'm ready for this page,
for this square of softening dirt,
for this garden of almost daffodils
to bang all my air to bells.

SKINKS

My friends and I arrived hungover
in that park beside the Potomac:
stagnant creeks, humidity, the leaves
too weary for wind. It was late afternoon
and I climbed a hill of granite
to find the five-lined skinks laid out
in the sun as if they'd fallen from the air.
But the skinks were fast and every grab
produced a crevice, a fault
in the seemingly solid world that would let
the lizards in. I must have looked
like a slow god up there — so large
I could destroy them, yet easily evaded —
all headache and shakes and breathless
cursing. When one of their tails broke off
in my fingers, I clambered down to show
my friends. It was unnaturally blue,
as if it had been dipped into sky,
and it was twitching, writhing in my palm
like a minor miracle, a sacrifice
made so the lizard could live. Already
the new tail was budding somewhere
in that inscrutable granite above me. This
is my clearest memory: The broken tail
kept dancing in the dirt even after
I crushed my cigarette out
on the bluest blame-free part of it.

PARTY

It was New Year's Eve and we'd been drinking —
old college friends converging
from across the country to a single lit-up window
eight floors high in a city of lit-up windows.
Some of them had blinds or gauzy curtains;
some were bare with the privacy that comes
from being seen only by people
you'd never be able to name. It had been years
since we'd had a drink together. We talked
about our cancers and failed marriages.
The second wives showed off their new tattoos.
It went on like that all night — the triumphs
of the present book-ended by the twin catastrophes
of the past and of the future. The apartment
had a telescope. In one window people were
fucking. In another they merely drank.
In others the strange blueness of the rooms
ignited by televisions. When it got late we opened
a bottle of champagne for each of us
and staggered to the roof. We knew it was
midnight by the cacophony of car horns
below us. The street was still packed with limousines
and cabs — all of them late for the year's biggest party.
A woman hung out of a passenger window
flashing some guys we couldn't see. Then fireworks
from somewhere started flickering the bricks
of the taller buildings that rose like the weather
around us. What happened next is gone forever,
though one of us may have tried for the street

before that woman could get away. We awoke
inside where the sugar ants were dying
in a puddle of vodka and cherry juice.
Someone had spilled it before throwing up
in a sinkful of drying dishes — and the ants
had found that too. Outside, the sun with its prybar
and siren was throbbing at the blinds.

TUESDAY NIGHT AT THE TRAVELING CIRCUS

Three tigers totter up
to their bright and tiny pedestals,
waiting to be told

by a sequined man
it's permissible to roar. One by one
he will try on a halo

of saliva and sparkling
teeth, and when the first mouth closes down,
it reeks of the raw

chuck steak
that keeps the big cat lazy. Almost
no one applauds

as he removes his head,
stepping forward to the next set of teeth
while waving

an immaculate glove.
For a moment it looks like he's conducting
the canned music

as it spills
into the bleachers from the black trumpets
of the sound system.

But the audience cares
nothing for the hoop of fire
that never burns,

for the whip
that impacts only itself
in the popcorned

and sawdusty air
of the tent. They came here to see the tame
untamed. Someone,

they seem to be saying,
had better get into that cage, and the cage
had better mean it.

That's how desperate
they are. They need something
to turn away from.

SEDUCTION

She has surrounded herself with broken
mirrors: rearviews and compacts
and full-length triptychs — whatever
you might use to get a sense of yourself
in the vast and punishing world.
Among the shards you find her
with a bracelet of barbed wire,
a pendant of living bees. She understands
suffering and possesses the bandage
she knows you need — already
primed with blood and kisses. Of course
she is beautiful. She reminds you
of berries in a whirlwind of thorns,
a suitcase full of cash that someone has pushed
to the center of the tiger's cage. She breaks
another mirror and sprinkles it like jimmies
over the pastry of her skin.
Come and get it, she seems to be saying.
You're worried that you will.

THE MAN WITH A GALLON OF GASOLINE

He could cut a dozen lawns or satisfy a lover
within a fourteen-mile radius — depending
on the car, and assuming he had to return
to the place his lover was not. He could make
some headway as an arsonist. He believes
he could burn down many buildings —
though he would have to ration, to create
the right kind of draft, to pick only homes
where the firehouse is far. If the revolution came,
he might have enough for an armful
of Molotov cocktails — to hold an alley
or to cook a tank. It's cool when he dips his finger in.
He lets some of it rainbow onto his driveway,
the fumes so powerful they bring us to war.
This is what an era smells like, he thinks,
digested by the planet, exhumed.
Maybe he should start a two-minute signal fire,
an SOS for the satellites and jets
that own the air above him. Or maybe
he should content himself with a week
of forgettable errands. It might be nice,
as long as he could live with the low-fuel icon
lit like the tip of a cigarette beside his left hand,
as long as he could live with the chance
of conking out on a road too far from home
for the ice cream to make it back.
He would have to eat it as he walked
down a heat-rippled street — scooping it out

by hand, soon to be followed by yellow wasps,
the flies so fast they cannot be killed.

PRELUDE

The moon ignited the window frost
as I searched the early snow:

the road unplowed, the car chloroformed,
the hemlock branches reaching down.

Inside, the plates stacked up like poker chips,
the knives and forks nested

in their slots, and the bathroom tile
was gleaming. I'd already made sure

the kitchen was loaded with wine
and marbled steak, and the bed lay taut

in the curtained dark beneath
its billowing quilt. The whole house felt

like a trigger or a gritty fuse.
It was ready for something

or anything: a dinner party, a love affair,
a visit from relatives, spring.

Meanwhile the page of the back-yard snow
had already been printed

with what lived wild among us.

ADRIFT

The woman who has learned to levitate
yanks her curtains shut, pulls a brass chain
across her door, and rises above
the dirty rug, the unmatched
pillows of her loveseat. She feels only
the pressure of her clothing, and so
the clothing comes off: her dress
and bra, the panties like a burst balloon.
She wafts along like a statue of smoke,
drifting up to where the air is warm —
floating on her back among the cornered
webs, the only paint in her apartment
free of fingerprints and scuffs. By now
her nipples have hardened into points
and she is touching herself with a tenderness
she didn't expect. But soon enough
the phone goes off like a little machine gun
firing bells. It is the man she tells
everyone she loves. He says that he is close
to her exit now, that she should be ready
when he arrives. The woman who can levitate
hangs up. She steps into the black sack
of her dress and tugs it into place,
pushes the lipstick over her mouth.
In the other room the door is locked,
the music of the chain still waiting for her touch.

THE MAN REMEMBERS THE ONLY
CUMMERBUND HE HAS EVER WORN

My date had a wrist corsage —
another first and last time confused
with brandy. Her dress belled around her
as if she'd stepped into an overturned
tulip, and my tuxedo was tight
in the shoulders, despite my having
been fitted. It is easy now to see her
innocence, the crassness of my own
desire. I cannot explain
how nudity is deepened
by the presence of a wrist corsage,
but she was careful not to crush it
as I peeled the stockings from her legs.
The cummerbund never made it back
to the rental shop. I left it
on the dock of a moonlit lake
as if the country I had conquered were
waiting for a flag. It stayed there
with her silence, which even now
I cannot hear. The clamor of it
terrifies on nights my daughter
is even just a little bit late.

BISMARCK

At the reunion, people said you'd ended up
in Bismarck after two marriages
to men who beat you raw. No one knew why.
Somebody said you had family there,
another a friend from college.
Or maybe you just ran out of timing
belt and cash on the city's frozen outskirts.
I remember your face, which I held
one Saturday night like a bird's nest
of balanced eggs by the light of the odometer
and radio dial. It was a softness against me
and I could tell even then how easily
it would break in the hands of a different man.
We were parked away from the last lamp
on Commerce Drive, and the forty minutes
between the end of the movie and the hour
of your curfew became a kind of bliss. Now
you're among the missing — a name
on a list printed on the back page
of the reunion directory. I can only hope
you've figured a way to become
the way you were, living in Bismarck —
a city named for the man
who founded a German empire,
for a battleship stalled at the bottom of a sea.

THE MAN OUT WALKING
ON THE STREETS OF NEW HAVEN

The streetlights come on at once —
their lamps brightening
beneath a starless November sky.

Everywhere the neon curls
of bar windows that haven't turned off in years,
and the dog that nobody pets

nosing into trash as it orbits the block
it was born on. The air is cold,
no one is out but the smokers and me.

Close by, a concrete-bottomed creek
is leaking something from a little higher up.
It is a long and unspectacular tumble

down the side of Connecticut —
clogged with suburbs and deer wire,
nail salons, drained swimming pools.

No woman has spoken to me in weeks
or held out her hand to save me
from the stars I cannot see

that somehow, I'm sure of it, are steering me.

THE MAN WATCHING BUMBLE BEES
IN THE SOUTH JERSEY PINE BARRENS

After walking fifteen miles into pitch pines,
I collapse in a clearing filled
with the oblong bells of blueberries
in flower. A half-dozen bees are mining them.
They never taste the same one twice
and they are methodical as they pull
the blossoms on like little bags. It is almost twilight.
The bees are fat and loud — louder,
at least, than the mourning dove
calling from a swamp that kisses the path
that carried me, louder than my blood
settling down after so many miles
of sugar sand, and louder than the F-16
dividing the sky with the chalk of its contrail
the way a teacher divides a blackboard
to begin a lesson. They seem almost frantic
as the sun dissolves behind a scrim
of needles and evening cloud — as if it had fallen
to these six bees to pollinate this patch
of horizoning berries. The fissure of honey
they have hidden in some log
must be draining into sand faster
than the blossoms can miracle out
of these twigs. It will be dark inside the hour —
the air black with the same night that hobbled
over Europe and the vast Atlantic.
The moon will not be up. I should be getting ready.

THE MAN CONTEMPLATING THE CLARITY
OF MIDWESTERN LAKE WATER

Friends had brought us to a beach of stone —
so foreign to us, having come from the Jersey shore —
no sand anywhere, a ledge of quartzite
flashing in the sun. And fresh water too —
the strangeness of opening eyes easily,
the lake small enough that its weather was
the weather of the town. The ocean had always been
a messenger: the storm headed in
from Africa, the syringes of someone dying
on Staten Island. But this lake water was green
and calm. What fish there were
were easily discerned, and none of them
could kill us — unless it was by choking
as we ate them from a pan. Lifeguards could forget
about this water whole minutes at a time.
It was quiet too — I remember listening to the oar shafts
grind against their oarlocks as a rowboat
dragged itself over reflected sky
forty yards from shore. The sound was deliberate,
relaxed, the way most people might hope
to sound at the crossroads of their lives.
We collapsed into lawn chairs hauled from a dirty trunk —
the sand of the distant Atlantic hissing
inside their aluminum frames, the same sun
scalding us where someone had nailed it
to the sky above our Monaco,
this water with a bottom that anyone can see.

THE MAN WAITING FOR THE BOAT TO STILL

It is cloudless and moonless and breezeless —
a night of deficiencies he has grown
to love. He has rowed himself out
in the only canoe left unchained beside the lake
that in summer was full of motorboats
and bikinis and sweating beers. It's November now,
and he's made his way to a corner
of the lake where there aren't any
houses along the shore, or else
their lights are off and everyone is curled
into their dreamless wine. He is waiting
for the boat to still itself. The stars are
sparking and blue, as if someone had
shotgunned the air with light. It's all
in the lake beneath him too, making him feel
like someone has slipped him inside
an envelope of infinity — like he's about to be
delivered. But the canoe keeps vibrating —
the water dripping from the oar is enough
to turn the lake pure black, to obliterate
the frozen stars that story his night
with monarchs and dogs. His shivering
doesn't help matters. It's only in the distance
that the world is sufficiently still to echo
that blueness back. He statues there for hours,
refusing to drift, overhearing the migration

of Canada geese blotting the stars
above him and below — a darkness
that is desperate to find someplace to stall,
to crash upon clear water that is welcoming and still.

MUSEUM

I dragged my fingernail across Picasso's signature,
taking a fleck of it with me. It's not
what you would call damage — just a gap
in the "o" where the brush might have skipped
as he signed his name in a flourish of nicotine.
The guard was busy pretending to watch someone else,
and I left in one of those museum elevators
that rise and fall without any noise
except for the chime of the opening door.
Then I was outside, among the twittering of finches
that kept disappearing in the newly planted elm crowns
destined to grow and die inside those squares
of sidewalk dirt. Back at home, I picked
the paint from underneath my nail
with a needle from my bachelor's sewing kit.
I dropped it, still sticking to the point,
inside an old prescription vial and placed it on a sill
overlooking an alley that led to the market
where the fish were dumped
each morning still wet with the sea. That sill was
a tiny museum. It held a crumb of bronze I'd scraped off
a Henry Moore while visiting a sculpture garden,
and the drywall screw I did it with. And a cigarette
Madonna had flicked into traffic on Eighth Avenue.
I nearly got killed collecting it, but it was burning
when I picked it up, and I sucked the last of it in —
her lipstick smudge the color of dawn,
the car horns letting me have it.
There's even something from today — a strand of hair

from the sweater of the woman I stood behind
on the escalator. I twined it around my finger
like a dock rope to haul her in,
but she kept going as we crested,
as easily as smoke leaving a fire on a mountaintop
married to furious wind. I am smoldering still
in my drapeless apartment, as the moon pours over
the collectable world — lonely and pretty and ready
to be taken. It says to get up, that the couch will drown me
if I don't, that everywhere the guards are sleepy
with beer and begging to be deceived.

THE MAN WHO WORRIED

He collected obscure ways of dying —
chimney fires and Ebola,
hot tub drownings, a man crushed
on a fishing boat deck
when the net gave way above him
and the mackerel waterfalled down.
His collection led to a certain way
of carrying himself, even
in mundane scenarios.
Every man had mayhem on his lips.
Every woman kept a derringer
or a meth habit at the bottom
of her purse. Even the supermarket
was a place to buy pork
he might undercook.
The end of his world was
everywhere — ubiquitous as air,
the moon that could crush him,
this very moment, as it fell
through the bedroom drapes.

ACKNOWLEDGMENTS

Versions of the following poems have been previously published, many times with different titles:

2River: "The Man Who Worried"; "Rock Collection"
The Adroit Journal: "The Man With a Missing Watch in Spring"; "On Being Asked If I'd Ever Been to Georgia"
Anti-: "Tuesday Night at the Traveling Circus"
Breakwater: "The Man With a Star on the Tip of Each Finger"; "Comet"
Caduceus: "The Man Describes the End of His Escape"
Citron Review: "The Man Remembers the Only Cummerbund He Has Ever Worn"
Coachella Review: "A Rapture That Followed August Rain"
Connecticut Review: "The Problem With Almanacs"; "The Man Contemplating the Clarity of Midwestern Lake Water"
Connecticut River Review: "Comet"; "The Man Whose Friends Had Risen"
Crush Anthology: "Seduction"
Dogwood: "Appetites"
Eclipse: "The Man Watching Bumble Bees in the South Jersey Pine Barrens"
Escape Into Life: "The Man on Break"; "The Ocean at the End of Our Street"; "The Ocean at the End of Our Street"; "The Man Describes the End of His Escape"; "The Man With a Cardinal in His Bedroom"
Fourth River: "The Rising"; "Love at the Stamford Transportation Center"
Freshwater: "The Man Laments the Bees That Didn't Sting"
Jelly Bucket: "Adrift"; "Lobster"; "Butcher"; "Bismarck"
Linebreak: "The Man With a Shirt of Fire"

The Literary Review: "The Man Waiting for the Boat to Still"; "The Man With a Boat at the Bottom of the Lake"; "The Man Who Enjoys Being Blackmailed"

Louisiana Literature: "The Man Describes Their Failed Vacation"; "The Disappearing Man"; "Family Vacation"; "The Man Beneath the January Stars"; "Prelude"

National Endowment for the Arts Writer's Corner: "Appetites"

The Newtowner: "The Man Who Is Ready"

The New Yorker: "The Man Explains His Souvenirs"

Paper Nautilus: "A Man Out Walking on the Streets of New Haven"

The Pedestal: "Descent"

Poems & Plays: "Theory"; "Museum"; "Seduction"; "The Man in Charge of Darkness"

Poetry.us.com: "Appetites"; "The Man With a Shirt on Fire"

Poetry East: "The Man With a Missing Dog"; "Skinks"

The Poetry Gymnasium: "Theory"

Pure Francis: "The Man With Rotten Fruit on His Wrist"

Southern Humanities Review: "The Lesson of Less Light"

The Southern Review: "The Man With a Hawk in His Suitcase"; "An Epiphany During the Morning Traffic on I-95"

Verse Daily: "The Man Waiting for the Boat to Still"; "The Man With a Boat at the Bottom of the Lake"

Xanadu: "A Man Out Walking on the Streets of New Haven"

Some of these poems appeared in a chapbook, *Appetites*, published by Clemson University Digital Press.

Thanks to BJ Ward for his close attention to these poems.

Thanks to the National Endowment for the Arts and to the Connecticut Commission on Culture & Tourism for their support, which enabled me to write and revise these poems.

CHARLES RAFFERTY has received grants from the National Endowment for the Arts and the Connecticut Commision on Culture & Tourism. This is his tenth collection of poetry. His poems have appeared widely, including *The New Yorker*, *Oprah Magazine*, *Poetry East*, *Louisiana Literature*, *The Literary Review*, and *The Southern Review*. He is also the author of a collection of short stories—*Saturday Night at Magellan's*. Currently, he directs the MFA program at Albertus Magnus College.